I *Should* be *Dead* by *Now*

A Hypochondriac's Guide to *Life*

hy·po·chon·dri·ac
ˌhīpəˈkändrēˌak/
noun
a person who is abnormally
anxious about their health.

Disclaimer:

For my benefit and yours, In this book, I'm only going to list the diseases & conditions and not provide the full definition for each one. There's a great chance that we may or may not currently have some if not most of these and if I add a description for each one, it's entirely possible that we may realize we actually have more ailments than first realized.

However, If you wish to learn more about any condition listed in this book, the internet can provide you with full descriptions and a symptom checker to confirm what you already know...
You *probably* already have it.
(Check at your own risk)

The following is a list from A-Z of all the Diseases & Conditions that the human body may have. For a hypochondriac you will probably be amazed at how many of these you have already had, currently have or will have at some point in the future.

A
Abdominal Aortic Aneurysm — see Aortic Aneurysm
Acanthamoeba Infection
ACE (Adverse Childhood Experiences)
Acinetobacter Infection
Acquired Immune Deficiency Syndrome (AIDS) — see HIV/AIDS
Acquired Immunodeficiency Syndrome (AIDS) — see HIV/AIDS
Adenovirus Infection
Adenovirus Vaccination
ADHD [Attention Deficit/Hyperactivity Disorder]
Adult Vaccinations
Adverse Childhood Experiences (ACE)
AFib, AF (Atrial fibrillation)
African Trypanosomiasis — see Sleeping Sickness
Agricultural Safety — see Farm Worker Injuries
AHF (Alkhurma hemorrhagic fever)
AIDS (Acquired Immune Deficiency Syndrome)
AIDS (Acquired Immunodeficiency Syndrome)
Alkhurma hemorrhagic fever (AHF)
ALS [Amyotrophic Lateral Sclerosis]
Alzheimer's Disease

Amebiasis, Intestinal [Entamoeba histolytica infection]

American Indian and Alaska Native Vaccination

American Trypanosomiasis — see Chagas Disease

Amphibians and Fish, Infections from — see Fish and Amphibians, Infections from

Amyotrophic Lateral Sclerosis — see ALS

Anaplasmosis, Human

Ancylostoma duodenale Infection, Necator americanus Infection — see Human Hookworm

Angiostrongylus Infection

Animal-Related Diseases

Anisakiasis — see Anisakis Infection

Anisakis Infection [Anisakiasis]

Anthrax [Bacillus anthracis Infection]

Antibiotic and Antimicrobial Resistance

Antibiotic Use, Appropriate
see also Get Smart about Antibiotics Week

Aortic Aneurysm

Aortic Dissection — see Aortic Aneurysm

Arenavirus Infection

Arthritis

Childhood Arthritis

Fibromyalgia

Gout

Osteoarthritis (OA)

Rheumatoid Arthritis (RA)

Ascariasis — see Ascaris Infection

Ascaris Infection [Ascariasis]

Aseptic Meningitis — see Viral Meningitis

Aspergillosis — see Aspergillus Infection

Aspergillus Infection [Aspergillosis]

Asthma
Atrial fibrillation (AFib, AF)
Attention Deficit/Hyperactivity Disorder — see ADHD
Autism
see also Genetics and Genomics
Avian Influenza

B
B virus Infection [Herpes B virus]
B. cepacia infection (Burkholderia cepacia Infection)
Babesia Infection — see Babesiosis
Babesiosis [Babesia Infection]
Bacillus anthracis — see Anthrax
Bacillus anthracis Infection — see Anthrax
Back Belts — see Ergonomic and Musculoskeletal Disorders
Bacterial Meningitis
see also Meningitis [Meningococcal Disease]
Bacterial Vaginosis (BV)
Balamuthia mandrillaris Infection — see Balamuthia Infection
Balamuthia Infection [Balamuthia mandrillaris Infection]
Balantidiasis — see Balantidium Infection
Balantidium Infection [Balantidiasis]
Bartonella bacilliformis Infection — see Carrión's disease
Bartonella quintana Infection — see Trench fever
Baylisascaris Infection — see Raccoon Roundworm Infection

BCG (Tuberculosis Vaccine)

Bilharzia — see Schistosomiasis

Bioterrorism Agents/Diseases

Bird Flu — see Avian Influenza

Birth Defects

Black Lung [Coal Workers' Pneumoconioses]

Blast Injuries

Blastocystis hominis Infection — see Blastocystis
Infection

Blastocystis Infection [Blastocystis hominis
Infection]

blood clot

Blood Disorders

Body Lice [Pediculus humanus corporis]

Borrelia burgdorferi Infection — see Lyme Disease

Botulism [Clostridium botulinum Infection]

Bovine Spongiform Encephalopathy (BSE)

Brainerd Diarrhea

Breast and Ovarian Cancer and Family Health
History

see also Breast and Ovarian Cancer and Family
Health History

Breast Cancer

see also National Breast and Cervical Cancer Early
Detection Program (NBCCEDP)

Breastfeeding

Bronchiolitis — see Respiratory Syncytial Virus
Infection

Bronchitis

Brucella Infection [Brucellosis]

Brucellosis — see Brucella Infection

BSE (Bovine Spongiform Encephalopathy)

BSE (Mad Cow Disease)
Burkholderia cepacia Infection (B. cepacia infection)
Burkholderia mallei — see Glanders
Burkholderia pseudomallei Infection — see Melioidosis
BV (Bacterial Vaginosis)

C
C. diff. Infection [Clostridium difficile Infection]
C. gattii cryptococcosis
C. neoformans cryptococcosis
Campylobacter Infection [Campylobacteriosis]
Campylobacteriosis — see Campylobacter Infection
Cancer
Colorectal (Colon) Cancer
Gynecologic Cancers
Lung Cancer
Prostate Cancer
Skin Cancer
see also Breast Cancer
Cancer and Flu
see also Cancer
see also Influenza
Cancer Health Disparities — see Health Disparities in Cancer
Candida Infection [Candidiasis]
Genital Candidiasis (VVC) [Vulvovaginal Candidiasis]
Invasive Candidiasis
Thrush [Oropharyngeal Candidiasis]

Candidiasis — see Candida Infection
Canine Flu
Capillaria Infection [Capillariasis]
Capillariasis — see Capillaria Infection
Carbapenem resistant Klebsiella pneumonia (CRKP) — see Klebsiella pneumoniae
Carbapenem-resistant Enterobacteriaceae (CRE)
Cardiovascular Health — see Heart Disease
Carpal Tunnel Syndrome — see Ergonomic and Musculoskeletal Disorders
Carrión's disease [Bartonella bacilliformis Infection]
Cat Flea Tapeworm — see Tapeworm, Dog and Cat Flea
Cat Scratch Disease from Pets
Cats, Infections from
CCHF (Crimean-Congo hemorrhagic fever)
CDI (Chronic Disease Indicators)
Cercarial Dermatitis — see Swimmer's Itch
Cerebral Palsy
Cervical Cancer
see also National Breast and Cervical Cancer Early Detection Program (NBCCEDP)
CFS (Chronic Fatigue Syndrome)
Chagas Disease [Trypanosoma cruzi Infection]
Chapare Hemorrhagic Fever (CHHF)
Chest Cold — see Bronchitis
CHHF (Chapare Hemorrhagic Fever)
Chickenpox [Varicella Disease]
Chickenpox Vaccination
Chikungunya Fever (CHIKV)
CHIKV (Chikungunya Fever)

Childhood Arthritis
Childhood Injuries
Childhood Overweight and Obesity
Children's Cough and Cold Medicines — see
Cough and Cold Medicines
Chlamydia [Chlamydia trachomatis Disease]
Chlamydia trachomatis Disease — see Chlamydia
Chlamydophila (Chlamydia) pneumoniae
Infection
Cholera [Vibrio cholerae Infection]
Chronic Disease Indicators (CDI)
Chronic Disease Prevention
Chronic Fatigue Syndrome (CFS)
Chronic Kidney Disease (CKD)
Chronic Obstructive Pulmonary Disease (COPD)
Chronic Wasting Disease (CWD)
Ciguatera Fish Poisoning
Ciguatoxin — see Marine Toxins
CJD, Classic (Classic Creutzfeldt-Jakob Disease)
CKD (Chronic Kidney Disease)
CKD (Kidney Disease)
Classic Creutzfeldt-Jakob Disease (CJD, Classic)
Clonorchiasis — see Clonorchis Infection
Clonorchis Infection [Clonorchiasis]
Clostridium botulinum Infection — see Botulism
Clostridium difficile Infection — see C. diff.
Infection
Clostridium perfringens infection
Clostridium tetani Infection — see Tetanus
Disease
Clotting Disorders
CMV (Cytomegalovirus Infection)

Coal Workers' Pneumoconioses — see Black Lung
Coccidioidomycosis — see Valley Fever
Cold, Common
Colorado Tick Fever (CTF)
Colorectal (Colon) Cancer
Colorectal Cancer Control Program (CRCCP)
Colorectal Cancer and Genetics
see also Colorectal (Colon) Cancer
see also Genetics and Genomics
Common Cold — see Cold, Common
Concussion — see Traumatic Brain Injury
Congenital Hearing Loss — see Hearing Loss in
Children
Congenital Heart Defects
Screening for Critical Congenital Heart Defects
Conjunctivitis — see Pink Eye
Cooley's Anemia
COPD (Chronic Obstructive Pulmonary Disease)
Corynebacterium diphtheriae Infection — see
Diphtheria
Cough and Cold Medicines
Coxiella burnetii Infection — see Q Fever
CRE (Carbapenem-resistant Enterobacteriaceae)
Creutzfeldt-Jakob Disease, Classic — see Classic
Creutzfeldt-Jakob Disease
Crimean-Congo hemorrhagic fever (CCHF)
[Nairovirus Infection]
CRKP (Carbapenem resistant Klebsiella
pneumonia)
Crohn's Disease — see Inflammatory Bowel
Disease
Cronobacter Infection

Cryptococcosis, C. gattii. — see C. gattii cryptococcosis

Cryptococcosis, C. neoformans — see C. neoformans cryptococcosis

Cryptosporidiosis — see Cryptosporidium Infection

Cryptosporidium Infection [Cryptosporidiosis]

CTF (Colorado Tick Fever)

CWD (Chronic Wasting Disease)

cyanobacterial algal bloom-associated illness — see Harmful Algal Bloom (HAB)-Associated Illness

Cyclospora Infection [Cyclosporiasis]

Cyclosporiasis — see Cyclospora Infection

Cysticercosis

Cystoisospora Infection [Cystoisosporiasis]

Cystoisosporiasis — see Cystoisospora Infection

Cytomegalovirus Infection (CMV)

D

Death, Leading Causes of Death in Males see also Mortality Data

Deep Vein Thrombosis (DVT)

Dengue Fever (DF)

Dengue Hemorrhagic Fever (DHF) — see Dengue Fever

Dermatophyte Infection — see Ringworm

Developmental Disabilities

DF (Dengue Fever)

DHF (Dengue Hemorrhagic Fever)

Diabetes

Dientamoeba fragilis Infection

Diet and Nutrition — see Nutrition

Diphtheria [Corynebacterium diphtheriae Infection]

Diphtheria Vaccination

Diphyllobothriasis — see Diphyllobothrium Infection

Diphyllobothrium Infection [Diphyllobothriasis]

Dipylidium Infection — see Tapeworm, Dog and Cat Flea

Dirofilariasis (Dog Heartworm)

Division of Public Health Systems and Workforce Development (DPHSWD)

Division of Public Health Systems and Workforce Development (DPHSWD) — see Division of Public Health Systems and Workforce Development

Dog Bites

Dog Flea Tapeworm — see Tapeworm, Dog and Cat Flea

Dog Heartworm [Dirofilaria] — see Dirofilariasis (Dog Heartworm)

Dogs, Infections from

Down Syndrome [Trisomy 21]

DPHSWD (Division of Public Health Systems and Workforce Development)

Dracunculiasis — see Guinea Worm Disease

Drug Resistance — see Antibiotic and Antimicrobial Resistance

DVT (Deep Vein Thrombosis)

Dwarf Tapeworm [Hymenolepis Infection]

E

E. coli Infection [Escherichia coli Infection]

Ear Infection [Otitis Media]
Early Hearing Detection and Intervention (EHDI)
— see Hearing, Early Detection & Intervention
Eastern Equine Encephalitis (EEE)
Ebola Virus Disease (EVD)
EBV Infection (Epstein-Barr Virus Infection)
Echinococcosis
EEE (Eastern Equine Encephalitis)
EHDI (Early Hearing Detection and Intervention)
Ehrlichiosis, Human
Elephantiasis — see Lymphatic Filariasis
Elizabethkingia Infection
Emerging Infectious Diseases
Endophthalmitis, Fungal — see Fungal Eye
Infections
Entamoeba histolytica infection — see Amebiasis,
Intestinal
Enteric Diseases from Animals — see
Gastrointestinal Diseases from Animals
Enterobius vermicularis Infection — see Pinworm
Infection
Enterovirus D68
Enterovirus Infections (Non-Polio) — see
Non-Polio Enterovirus Infections
Epidemic Typhus — see Typhus Fevers
Epilepsy
Epstein-Barr Virus Infection (EBV Infection)
Ergonomic and Musculoskeletal Disorders
Escherichia coli Infection — see E. coli Infection
Esophageal Candidiasis — see Thrush
EV-D68 — see Enterovirus D68
EVD (Ebola Virus Disease)

Exserohilum rostratum (Other Pathogenic Fungi)
see also Fungal diseases [Mycotic diseases]
Extensively Drug-Resistant TB (XDR TB)
Extreme Cold [Hypothermia]
Extreme Heat [Hyperthermia]

F
Falls from Elevation
Falls, Older Adults
Family Health
Family Health History
Family Health History and Breast and Ovarian
Cancer — see Breast and Ovarian Cancer and
Family Health History
Farm Animals, Infections from
Farm Worker Injuries
see also Cost-effective Rollover Protective
Structures (CROPS)
Fasciitis, Necrotizing — see Group A Strep
Infection
Fasciola Infection [Fascioliasis]
Fascioliasis — see Fasciola Infection
Fasciolopsiasis — see Fasciolopsis Infection
Fasciolopsis Infection [Fasciolopsiasis]
Fetal Alcohol Spectrum Disorder
FETP — see Field Epidemiology Training Program
FETP (Field Epidemiology Training Program)
Fibromyalgia
Field Epidemiology Training Program (FETP)
Fifth Disease [Parvovirus B19 Infection]
Filariasis, Lymphatic — see Lymphatic Filariasis
Fish and Amphibians, Infections from

Flavorings-Related Lung Disease
Flu — see Influenza
Flu and Cancer — see Cancer and Flu
Flu Vaccination — see Influenza Vaccination
Flu, Pandemic — see Pandemic Flu
Flu, Seasonal — see Seasonal Flu
Folliculitis — see Hot Tub Rash
Food Poisoning — see Foodborne Illness
Food-Related Diseases
Clostridium perfringens infection
Shigella Infection [Shigellosis]
Foodborne Illness
Fragile X Syndrome (FXS)
Francisella tularensis Infection — see Tularemia
Fungal diseases [Mycotic diseases]
C. gattii cryptococcosis
C. neoformans cryptococcosis
Candida Infection [Candidiasis]
Histoplasma capsulatum Infection
[Histoplasmosis]
Aspergillus Infection [Aspergillosis]
Blastomycosis [Blastomyces dermatitidis
Infection]
Blastomycosis [Blastomyces dermatitidis infection]
Fungal Eye Infections
Histoplasmosis [Histoplasma capsulatum
Infection]
Mucormycosis
Pneumocystis pneumonia (PCP) [Pneumocystis
jirovecii pneumonia (previously Pneumocystis
carinii)]
Ringworm [Dermatophyte Infection]

Sporotrichosis
Sporotrichosis [Sporothrix schenckii infection]
Valley Fever [Coccidioidomycosis]
see also Mold
Fungal Eye Infections
Fungal Meningitis
see also Meningitis [Meningococcal Disease]
Fungal Pneumonia — see Valley Fever
FXS (Fragile X Syndrome)

G
GAE (Acanthamoeba) (Granulomatous Amebic
Encephalitis (Acanthamoeba))
GAE (Granulomatous amebic encephalitis)
GAS (Group A Strep Infection)
Gastrointestinal Diseases from Animals [Zoonotic
enteric diseases]
GBS (Group B Strep Infection)
GBS and Menactra Meningococcal Vaccine — see
Guillain-Barré Syndrome and Menactra
Meningococcal Vaccine
GDDER (Global Disease Detection and Emergency
Response)
Genetics and Colorectal Cancer — see Colorectal
Cancer and Genetics
Genetics and Heart Disease — see Heart Disease
and Genetics
Genetics and Mental Health — see Mental Health
and Genetics
Genetics and Obesity — see Obesity and Genetics
Genetics and Skin Cancer — see Skin Cancer and
Genetics

Genetics and Stroke — see Stroke and Genetics
Genital Candidiasis (VVC) [Vulvovaginal
Candidiasis]
Genital Herpes [Herpes Simplex Virus Infection]
Genital Warts — see Human Papillomavirus
Infection
German Measles (Rubella Virus)
Giardia Infection [Giardiasis]
Giardiasis — see Giardia Infection
Glanders [Burkholderia mallei]
Global Disease Detection and Emergency
Response (GDDER)
Global Health Security
see also Global Health
Global Measles Elimination
see also Global Health
see also Global Measles Elimination
see also Immunization
see also Measles
see also Measles Vaccination
Gnathostoma Infection — see Gnathostomiasis
Gnathostomiasis [Gnathostoma Infection]
Gonorrhea [Neisseria gonorrhoeae Infection]
Gout
Granulomatous amebic encephalitis (GAE) — see
Balamuthia Infection
Granulomatous Amebic Encephalitis
(Acanthamoeba) (GAE (Acanthamoeba)) — see
Acanthamoeba Infection
Group A Strep Infection (GAS) [Group A
Streptococcal Infection]

Group A Streptococcal Infection — see Group A Strep Infection

Group B Strep Infection (GBS) [Group B Streptococcal Infection]

Group B Streptococcal Infection — see Group B Strep Infection

Guillain-Barré Syndrome and Menactra Meningococcal Vaccine

Guinea Worm Disease [Dracunculiasis]

Gynecologic Cancers

Cervical Cancer

Ovarian Cancer

Uterine Cancer

Vaginal and Vulvar Cancers

H

H3N2v influenza

see also Variant Viruses - see Influenza

H5N1 — see Avian Influenza

HAB (Harmful Algal Bloom (HAB)-Associated Illness)

Haemophilus influenzae Infection (including Hib Infection)

Haemophilus influenzae Serotype b — see Hib Infection

Hand, Foot, and Mouth Disease (HFMD)

Hansen's Disease

Hantavirus Pulmonary Syndrome (HPS)

Harmful Algal Bloom (HAB)-Associated Illness (HAB)

Hazardous Drug Exposures in Healthcare

Head Lice [Pediculus humanus capitis]

Health Disparities in Cancer

Health Disparities in HIV/AIDS, Viral Hepatitis, STDs, and TB

Health Security — see Global Health Security

Healthcare Associated Infections

surgical site infection (SSI)

Healthy Pets, Healthy People — see Animal-Related Diseases

Healthy Weight

Hearing impairment — see Hearing loss, environmental

Hearing Loss in Children

Hearing loss, environmental [Hearing impairment]

Hearing, Early Detection & Intervention

Heart Disease [Cardiovascular Health]

Heart Disease and Genetics

see also Genetics and Genomics

see also Heart Disease [Cardiovascular Health]

see also Heart Disease Awareness

Heat Stress

Hemoglobinopathies

Hemophilia

Hemophilia Treatment Centers (HTC)

Hemorrhagic Fevers, Viral — see Viral Hemorrhagic Fevers

Hendra Virus Disease (HeV Infection)

Hepatitis A Vaccination

Hepatitis B Vaccination

Hepatitis, Viral — see Viral Hepatitis

Hereditary Bleeding Disorders — see Hemophilia

Herpes B virus — see B virus Infection

Herpes Simplex Virus Infection — see Genital Herpes

Herpes Zoster — see Shingles

Herpes Zoster Vaccination — see Shingles Vaccination

Herpes, Genital — see Genital Herpes

Herpesvirus B — see B virus Infection

Herpesvirus simiae — see B virus Infection

Heterophyes Infection [Heterophyiasis]

Heterophyiasis — see Heterophyes Infection

HeV Infection (Hendra Virus Disease)

HFMD (Hand, Foot, and Mouth Disease)

Hib Infection [Haemophilus influenzae Serotype b]

Hib Vaccine (Haemophilus influenzae Serotype b Vaccination)

High Blood Pressure

Histoplasma capsulatum Infection [Histoplasmosis]

Histoplasmosis — see Histoplasma capsulatum Infection

HIV/AIDS

HIV/AIDS and STDs

Hookworm, Human [Ancylostoma duodenale Infection, Necator americanus Infection] — see Human Hookworm

Hookworm, Zoonotic — see Zoonotic Hookworm

Horses, Infections from

Hot Tub Rash [Pseudomonas dermatitis Infection]

HPIV (Human Parainfluenza Viruses)

HPS (Hantavirus Pulmonary Syndrome)

HPV Infection (Human Papillomavirus Infection)

HPV Vaccination (Human Papillomavirus
Vaccination)
HPV-Associated Cancers
HTC (Hemophilia Treatment Centers)
Human Ehrlichiosis — see Ehrlichiosis, Human
Human Hookworm [Ancylostoma duodenale
Infection, Necator americanus Infection]
Human Immunodeficiency Virus — see
HIV/AIDS
Human Papillomavirus Infection (HPV Infection)
Human Papillomavirus Vaccination (HPV
Vaccination)
Human Parainfluenza Viruses (HPIV)
Hymenolepis Infection — see Dwarf Tapeworm
Hypertension — see High Blood Pressure
Hyperthermia — see Extreme Heat
Hypothermia — see Extreme Cold

I
IBD (Inflammatory Bowel Disease)
IMMPaCt (International Micronutrient
Malnutrition Prevention and Control Program) —
see Micronutrient Malnutrition
Impetigo — see Group A Strep Infection
including Hib Infection (Haemophilus influenzae
Infection)
Infectious Mononucleosis — see Epstein-Barr
Virus Infection
Infertility
Inflammatory Bowel Disease (IBD)
Influenza
H1N1 Flu

People at High Risk
Seasonal Flu
Swine Influenza
see also H7N9 Influenza
see also Influenza
Influenza and Cancer — see Cancer and Flu
Influenza in Pigs — see Swine Influenza
Influenza Vaccination
Influenza, Avian — see Avian Influenza
Influenza, Pandemic — see Pandemic Flu
Injury, Healthy Swimming and Recreational Water
International Micronutrient Malnutrition Prevention & Control Program (IMMPaCt) — see Micronutrient Malnutrition
Intestinal Amebae Infection, Nonpathogenic — see Nonpathogenic (Harmless) Intestinal Protozoa
Invasive Candidiasis
Isospora Infection [Isosporiasis] — see Cystoisospora Infection

J
Japanese Encephalitis (JE)
Japanese Encephalitis (JE) Vaccination
Jaundice — see Newborn Jaundice
JE (Japanese Encephalitis)
JE (Japanese Encephalitis) Vaccination

K
K. pneumoniae (Klebsiella pneumoniae)
Kala-Azar — see Leishmania Infection
Kawasaki Disease (KD)

Kawasaki Syndrome — see Kawasaki Disease
KD (Kawasaki Disease)
Keratitis, Acanthamoeba — see Acanthamoeba Infection
Keratitis, Fungal — see Fungal Eye Infections
Kernicterus — see Newborn Jaundice
KFD (Kyasanur Forest disease)
Kidney Disease (CKD)
Klebsiella pneumoniae (K. pneumoniae)
Kyasanur Forest disease (KFD)

L
La Crosse Encephalitis (LAC)
La Crosse Encephalitis virus (LACV) — see La Crosse Encephalitis
LAC (La Crosse Encephalitis)
LACV (La Crosse Encephalitis virus)
Lassa Fever
Latex Allergies
LCM (Lymphocytic Choriomeningitis)
Lead Poisoning
Legionellosis — see Legionnaires' Disease
Legionnaires' Disease [Legionellosis]
Leishmania Infection [Leishmaniasis]
Leishmaniasis — see Leishmania Infection
Leprosy — see Hansen's Disease
Leptospira Infection [Leptospirosis]
Leptospirosis — see Leptospira Infection
Lice
Lice, Body — see Body Lice
Lice, Head — see Head Lice
Lice, Pubic — see Pubic Lice

Listeria Infection [Listeriosis]
Listeriosis — see Listeria Infection
Liver Disease and Hepatitis — see Viral Hepatitis
Loa loa Infection — see Loiasis
Lockjaw — see Tetanus Disease
Lockjaw Vaccination — see Tetanus (Lockjaw) Vaccination
Loiasis [Loa loa Infection]
Lou Gehrig's Disease — see ALS
LUHF (Lujo Hemorrhagic Fever)
Lujo Hemorrhagic Fever (LUHF)
Lung Cancer
Lupus (SLE) [Systemic lupus erythematosus]
Lyme Disease [Borrelia burgdorferi Infection]
Lymphatic Filariasis
Lymphedema — see Lymphatic Filariasis
Lymphocytic Choriomeningitis (LCM)

M
MAC (Mycobacterium avium Complex)
Mad Cow Disease (BSE) — see Bovine Spongiform Encephalopathy
Malaria
Marburg Hemorrhagic Fever
Marine Toxins
MD (Muscular Dystrophy)
MDR TB (Multidrug-Resistant TB)
Measles
Measles Vaccination
Melioidosis [Burkholderia pseudomallei Infection]
Men's Health
Meningitis

see also Meningitis
Meningococcal Disease
Meningococcal Vaccination
Mental Health
Mental Health and Genetics
see also Genetics and Genomics
see also Mental Health
Mental Retardation
MERS-CoV (Middle East Respiratory Syndrome Coronavirus)
Methicillin Resistant Staphylococcus aureus — see MRSA
microalgal bloom-associated illness — see Harmful Algal Bloom (HAB)-Associated Illness
Microcephaly
see also Zika Virus Infection
see also Zika Virus Infection and Pregnancy
Micronutrient Malnutrition
Microsporidia Infection
Middle East Respiratory Syndrome Coronavirus (MERS-CoV)
see also Coronavirus (CoV)
MMR Vaccination
Molluscum Contagiosum
Monkey B virus — see B virus Infection
Monkeypox
Monkeypox Vaccination
Mononucleosis, Infectious — see Epstein-Barr Virus Infection
Motor Vehicle Injuries
Mouse and Rat Control — see Rodents, Diseases from

MRSA [Methicillin Resistant Staphylococcus aureus]
Mucormycosis
Mucus — see Cold, Common
Multidrug-Resistant TB (MDR TB)
Multiple organ dysfunction syndrome — see Sepsis
Mumps
Mumps Vaccination
Muscular Dystrophy (MD)
Musculoskeletal Disorders — see Ergonomic and Musculoskeletal Disorders
Mycobacterium abscessus Infection
Mycobacterium avium Complex (MAC)
Mycobacterium tuberculosis Infection — see Tuberculosis
Mycoplasma pneumoniae Infection
Mycotic diseases — see Fungal diseases
Myelomeningocele — see Spina Bifida
Myiasis

N
Naegleria Infection [Primary Amebic Meningoencephalitis (PAM)]
Nairovirus Infection — see Crimean-Congo hemorrhagic fever
National Amyotrophic Lateral Sclerosis (ALS) Registry — see ALS
Necrotizing Fasciitis — see Group A Strep Infection
Neglected Tropical Diseases (NTD)
Neisseria gonorrhoeae Infection — see Gonorrhea

Pneumocystis jirovecii pneumonia (previously
Pneumocystis carinii) — see Pneumocystis
pneumonia
Neurocysticercosis — see Cysticercosis
Newborn Hearing — see Hearing, Early Detection
& Intervention
Newborn Jaundice [Kernicterus]
Nocardia asteroides Infection — see Nocardiosis
Nocardiosis [Nocardia asteroides Infection]
noise exposure — see Hearing loss, environmental
noise, environmental — see Hearing loss,
environmental
noise, recreational — see Hearing loss,
environmental
Non-Polio Enterovirus Infections
Nonpathogenic (Harmless) Intestinal Protozoa
Norovirus Infection
Norwalk-like Viruses (NLV) — see Norovirus
Infection
NTD (Neglected Tropical Diseases)

O
OA (Osteoarthritis)
Obesity and Genetics
Obesity and Overweight
Obesity and Overweight, Childhood — see
Childhood Overweight and Obesity
Occupational Cancers
Occupational Skin Conditions — see Skin
Conditions, Occupational
Occupational Stress — see Stress, Occupational
OHF (Omsk hemorrhagic fever)

Omsk hemorrhagic fever (OHF)
Onchocerciasis — see River Blindness
Opisthorchis Infection
Oral Cancer
Orf Virus Infection — see Sore Mouth Infection
Oropharyngeal Candidiasis — see Thrush
Oroya fever — see Carrión's disease
Osteoarthritis (OA)
Otitis Media — see Ear Infection
Outbreaks
Ovarian and Breast Cancer and Family Health History — see Breast and Ovarian Cancer and Family Health History
Ovarian Cancer
Overweight and Obesity — see Obesity and Overweight
Overweight and Obesity, Childhood — see Childhood Overweight and Obesity

P
PAD (Peripheral Arterial Disease)
Pandemic Flu
see also Influenza
Paragonimiasis — see Paragonimus Infection
Paragonimus Infection [Paragonimiasis]
Parainfluenza — see Human Parainfluenza Viruses
Parasitic Diseases
Parvovirus B19 Infection — see Fifth Disease
PCP (Pneumocystis pneumonia)
PCV (Pneumococcal Conjugate Vaccine)
PE (Pulmonary Embolism)

Pedestrian Injury
Pediculus humanus capitis — see Head Lice
Pediculus humanus corporis — see Body Lice
Pelvic Inflammatory Disease (PID)
Peripheral Arterial Disease (PAD)
Peripheral Arterial Insufficiency — see Peripheral Arterial Disease
Peripheral Arterial Occlusive Disease — see Peripheral Arterial Disease
Peripheral Vascular Disease — see Peripheral Arterial Disease
Pertussis (Whooping Cough)
Pertussis (Whooping Cough) Vaccination
Pet-Related Diseases — see Animal-Related Diseases
Phthiriasis — see Pubic Lice
PID (Pelvic Inflammatory Disease)
Pigs, Influenza in — see Swine Influenza
Pink Eye [Conjunctivitis]
Pinworm Infection [Enterobius vermicularis Infection]
Plague [Yersinia pestis Infection]
Pneumococcal Conjugate Vaccine (PCV)
Pneumococcal Disease
Pneumococcal Polysaccharide Vaccine (PPV)
Pneumoconioses, Coal Workers' — see Black Lung
Pneumocystis carinii Pneumonia (PCP) Infection — see Pneumocystis pneumonia
Pneumocystis pneumonia (PCP) [Pneumocystis jirovecii pneumonia (previously Pneumocystis carinii)]
Pneumonia

Polio Infection [Poliomyelitis Infection]
Polio Vaccination [Poliomyelitis Vaccination]
Poliomyelitis Infection — see Polio Infection
Poliomyelitis Vaccination — see Polio Vaccination
Pontiac Fever — see Legionnaires' Disease
Powassan (POW) virus
Poxvirus Infections
PPV (Pneumococcal Polysaccharide Vaccine)
Pregnancy
Primary Amebic Meningoencephalitis (PAM) —
see Naegleria Infection
Prion Diseases (TSEs) [Transmissible spongiform
encephalopathies]
Prostate Cancer
Pseudomonas aeruginosa Infection
Pseudomonas dermatitis Infection — see Hot Tub
Rash
Psittacosis
Psoriasis
Pubic Lice [Phthiriasis]
Pulmonary Embolism (PE) — see Deep Vein
Thrombosis
Pulmonary Hypertension

Q
Q Fever [Coxiella burnetii Infection]

R
RA (Rheumatoid Arthritis)
Rabies
Rabies Vaccination

Raccoon Roundworm Infection [Baylisascaris Infection]

Rat-Bite Fever (RBF) [Streptobacillus moniliformis Infection]

RBF (Rat-Bite Fever)

Recalled Vaccines

Recreational Water Illness (RWI)

Reptiles, Infections from

Respiratory Syncytial Virus Infection (RSV)

Rheumatoid Arthritis (RA)

Rickettsia rickettsii Infection — see Rocky Mountain Spotted Fever

Rickettsia, Spotted Fever Group — see Spotted Fever Group Rickettsia

Rickettsial Diseases

Rift Valley Fever (RVF)

Ringworm [Dermatophyte Infection]

Ringworm from Animals

River Blindness [Onchocerciasis]

RMSF (Rocky Mountain Spotted Fever)

Rocky Mountain Spotted Fever (RMSF) [Rickettsia rickettsii Infection]

Rodent Control — see Rodents, Diseases from

Rodents — see Rat-Bite Fever

Rodents, Diseases from

Rotavirus Infection

Rotavirus Vaccination

RSV (Respiratory Syncytial Virus Infection)

Rubella (German Measles) Vaccination

Rubeola — see Measles

Runny Nose — see Cold, Common

RVF (Rift Valley Fever)

RWI (Recreational Water Illness)

S
Salmonella typhi infection — see Typhoid Fever
Salmonella Infection [Salmonellosis]
Salmonella Infection from Animals
Salmonellosis — see Salmonella Infection
Salt
see also Heart Disease [Cardiovascular Health]
see also High Blood Pressure
Sappinia diploidea and Sappinia pedata — see
Sappinia Infection
Sappinia Infection [Sappinia diploidea and
Sappinia pedata]
SARS [Severe Acute Respiratory Syndrome]
Scabies
Scarlet Fever
Schistosoma Infection — see Schistosomiasis
Schistosomiasis [Schistosoma Infection]
Seasonal Flu
Sepsis [Septicemia]
Septic shock — see Sepsis
Septicemia — see Sepsis
Severe Acute Respiratory Syndrome — see SARS
Sexually Transmitted Disease Surveillance Reports
Sexually Transmitted Diseases (STDs)
  Bacterial Vaginosis (BV)
  Chlamydia [Chlamydia trachomatis Disease]
  Genital Herpes [Herpes Simplex Virus Infection]
  Gonorrhea [Neisseria gonorrhoeae Infection]
  Human Papillomavirus Infection (HPV Infection)
  Pelvic Inflammatory Disease (PID)

Syphilis [Treponema pallidum Infection]
Trichomoniasis [Trichomonas Infection]
see also HIV/AIDS and STDs
SFGR (Spotted Fever Group Rickettsia)
Shiga toxin-producing E. coli (STEC) — see E. coli Infection
Shigella Infection [Shigellosis]
Shigellosis — see Shigella Infection
Shingles [Varicella Zoster Virus (VZV)]
Shingles Vaccination
Sickle Cell Disease
SIDS (Sudden Infant Death Syndrome)
Sinus Infection [Sinusitis]
Sinusitus — see Sinus Infection
Skin Cancer
Skin Cancer and Genetics
see also Family History
see also Genetics and Genomics
see also Skin Cancer
Skin Conditions, Occupational
SLE (Lupus)
Sleep and Sleep Disorders
Sleeping Sickness [African Trypanosomiasis]
Smallpox
Smoking and Tobacco Use
Sodium — see Salt
Soil Transmitted Helminths
Sore Mouth Infection [Orf Virus Infection]
Sore Throat
Southern Tick-Associated Rash Illness (STARI)
Spina Bifida [Myelomeningocele]
Spirillum minus Infection — see Rat-Bite Fever

Sporothrix schenckii infection — see Sporotrichosis

Sporotrichosis [Sporothrix schenckii infection]

Spotted Fever Group Rickettsia (SFGR)

Staph — see Staphylococcus aureus Infection

Staphylococcus aureus Infection

STARI (Southern Tick-Associated Rash Illness)

STDs (Sexually Transmitted Diseases)

STDs and HIV/AIDS — see HIV/AIDS and STDs

STEC (Shiga toxin-producing E. coli)

Strep Infection, Group A — see Group A Strep Infection

Strep Infection, Group B — see Group B Strep Infection

Strep Throat — see Sore Throat

Streptobacillus moniliformis Infection — see Rat-Bite Fever

Streptococcus pneumoniae Infection

Stress, Occupational

Stroke

Stroke and Genetics

see also Genetics and Genomics

see also Stroke

Strongyloidiasis — see Strongyloidiasis - see Strongyloides Infection

Strongyloidiasis - see Strongyloides Infection [Strongyloidiasis]

Sudden Infant Death Syndrome (SIDS)

Surveillance Reports, Sexually Transmitted Disease — see Sexually Transmitted Disease Surveillance Reports

Swimmer's Itch [Cercarial Dermatitis]

Swimming-related Illness — see Recreational
Water Illness
Swine Influenza
Symptom Relief for Upper Respiratory Infections
Syphilis [Treponema pallidum Infection]
Systemic lupus erythematosus — see Lupus

T
Taenia Infection — see Tapeworm Infection
Tapeworm Infection [Taenia Infection]
Tapeworm, Dog and Cat Flea [Dipylidium
Infection]
TB (Tuberculosis)
TB (Tuberculosis) Vaccination
TB and HIV Coinfection
TB and the African-American Communtiy
TB Data & Statistics
TB Education and Training Network
TB in African-Americans — see TB and the
African-American Communtiy
TB Surveillance Reports — see TB Data & Statistics
TB Testing & Diagnosis
TBI (Traumatic Brain Injury)
Testicular Cancer
Tetanus (Lockjaw) Infection
Tetanus (Lockjaw) Vaccination
Tetanus Disease [Clostridium tetani Infection]
Thalassemia — see Cooley's Anemia
Thoracic Aortic Aneurysm — see Aortic
Aneurysm
Throat, Sore — see Sore Throat
Throat, Strep — see Sore Throat

Thrombophilia — see Clotting Disorders
Thrombosis — see Clotting Disorders
Thrush [Oropharyngeal Candidiasis]
Tickborne Diseases — see Ticks
Ticks
Anaplasmosis, Human
Babesiosis [Babesia Infection]
Ehrlichiosis, Human
Lyme Disease [Borrelia burgdorferi Infection]
Powassan (POW) virus
Rocky Mountain Spotted Fever (RMSF) [Rickettsia rickettsii Infection]
Southern Tick-Associated Rash Illness (STARI)
Tularemia [Francisella tularensis Infection]
Tinea — see Ringworm
Tobacco Use, Smoking and — see Smoking and Tobacco Use
Tourette Syndrome (TS)
Toxocara Infection — see Toxocariasis
Toxocariasis [Toxocara Infection]
Toxoplasma Infection — see Toxoplasmosis
Toxoplasmosis [Toxoplasma Infection]
Trachoma Infection
Transmissible spongiform encephalopathies — see Prion Diseases
Traumatic Brain Injury (TBI)
Traumatic Occupational Injuries
Trench fever [Bartonella quintana Infection]
Treponema pallidum Infection — see Syphilis
Trichinellosis (Trichinosis)
Trichomonas Infection — see Trichomoniasis
Trichomoniasis [Trichomonas Infection]

Trichuriasis — see Whipworm Infection
Trisomy 21 — see Down Syndrome
Trypanosoma cruzi Infection — see Chagas
Disease
Trypanosomiasis, African — see Sleeping Sickness
TS (Tourette Syndrome)
TSEs (Prion Diseases)
Tuberculosis (TB) [Mycobacterium tuberculosis
Infection]
Tuberculosis (TB) Vaccination
Tuberculosis and HIV Coinfection — see TB and
HIV Coinfection
Tuberculosis Skin Test — see TB Testing &
Diagnosis
Tuberculosis Training — see TB Education and
Training Network
Tuberculosis Vaccine (BCG)
Tularemia [Francisella tularensis Infection]
see also Ticks
Typhoid Fever [Salmonella typhi infection]
Typhoid Fever Vaccination
Typhus Fevers

U
Ulcerative Colitis — see Inflammatory Bowel
Disease
Undulant Fever — see Brucella Infection
Unexplained Respiratory Disease Outbreaks
(URDO)
Universal Newborn Hearing Screening — see
Hearing, Early Detection & Intervention

Upper Respiratory Infection Symptom Relief —
see Symptom Relief for Upper Respiratory
Infections
URDO (Unexplained Respiratory Disease
Outbreaks)
Uterine Cancer

V
Vaccination, American Indian and Alaska Native
— see American Indian and Alaska Native
Vaccination
Vaginal and Vulvar Cancers
Vaginal Candidiasis — see Genital Candidiasis
Valley Fever [Coccidioidomycosis]
Vancomycin-Intermediate/Resistant
Staphylococcus aureus Infections [VISA/VRSA]
Vancomycin-resistant Enterococci Infection (VRE)
Variant Creutzfeldt-Jakob Disease (vCJD)
Variant Viruses - see Influenza
Varicella Disease — see Chickenpox
Varicella Vaccination — see Chickenpox
Vaccination
Varicella Zoster Virus (VZV) — see Shingles
Varicella-Zoster Virus Infection
Variola Major Virus Infection — see Smallpox
Variola Minor Virus Infection — see Smallpox
vCJD (Variant Creutzfeldt-Jakob Disease)
verruga peruana — see Carrión's disease
VHF (Viral Hemorrhagic Fevers)
Vibrio cholerae Infection — see Cholera
Vibrio Illness [Vibriosis]
Vibriosis — see Vibrio Illness

Viral Hemorrhagic Fevers (VHF)
Alkhurma hemorrhagic fever (AHF)
Chapare Hemorrhagic Fever (CHHF)
Crimean-Congo hemorrhagic fever (CCHF)
[Nairovirus Infection]
Ebola Virus Disease (EVD)
Hantavirus Pulmonary Syndrome (HPS)
Kyasanur Forest disease (KFD)
Lassa Fever
Lujo Hemorrhagic Fever (LUHF)
Marburg Hemorrhagic Fever
Omsk hemorrhagic fever (OHF)
Rift Valley Fever (RVF)
Viral Hepatitis
Viral Meningitis [Aseptic Meningitis]
see also Meningitis [Meningococcal Disease]
VISA/VRSA — see
Vancomycin-Intermediate/Resistant
Staphylococcus aureus Infections
Vision Impairment
Von Willebrand Disease — see VWD
VRE (Vancomycin-resistant Enterococci Infection)
Vulvovaginal Candidiasis — see Genital
Candidiasis
VVC (Genital Candidiasis)
VWD [Von Willebrand Disease]
VZV (Varicella Zoster Virus) — see Shingles

W
Weight, Healthy — see Healthy Weight
West Nile Virus Infection (WNV Infection)
Whipworm Infection [Trichuriasis]

Whitmore's Disease — see Melioidosis
Whooping Cough — see Pertussis (Whooping Cough)
Whooping Cough (Pertussis) Vaccination
Wildlife, Infections from
Winter Storms — see Extreme Cold
WNV Infection (West Nile Virus Infection)
Women's Bleeding Disorders
Women's Health

X
XDR TB (Extensively Drug-Resistant TB)
Xenotropic Murine Leukemia Virus-related Virus Infection — see XMRV Infection
XMRV Infection [Xenotropic Murine Leukemia Virus-related Virus Infection]

Y
Yeast Infection — see Genital Candidiasis
Yellow Fever
Yellow Fever Vaccination
Yersinia enterocolitica Infection — see Yersiniosis
Yersinia pestis Infection — see Plague
Yersiniosis [Yersinia enterocolitica Infection]

Z
Zika Virus Infection
Zoonotic Diseases from Animals — see Animal-Related Diseases
Zoonotic enteric diseases — see Gastrointestinal Diseases from Animals
Zoonotic Hookworm

Zoster — see Shingles
Zygomycosis — see Mucormycosis

*This book is not intended to diagnose or treat any
injury or illness. If you think you have a serious
injury or illness contact your healthcare provider.

Now that you have made it through the very long and extensive list, I don't know whether to say "Congratulations" or "I'm Sorry".

I'm sure you have many questions and probably have an even longer list of diseases to search online so I won't keep you any longer. From one hypochondriac to another, I wish you health, happiness and the reassurance that more than likely everything will be ok, despite what that voice in your head is telling you right this moment.

Printed by Amazon Italia Logistica S.r.l.
Torrazza Piemonte (TO), Italy